GITANJALI

Rabindranath Tagore

GITANJALI

With Introduction,
Opening Notes and Illustrations

Introduction: Dr Yeats

Opening Notes: Dr George Kaitholil

Illustrations: Sr Solange

BETTER YOURSELF BOOKS

ISBN 81-7108-446-X

Cover: Manoj Pal

3rd Print **2003**

Website: www.stpaulsbyb.com
E-mail: marketing@stpaulsbyb.com

Printed by Dominic V.
at St Paul Press Training School, Bandra
and published by BETTER YOURSELF BOOKS,
23rd Road, TPS III, Bandra, Mumbai 400 050
2003

INTRODUCTION

A few days ago I said to a distinguished Bengali doctor of medicine, "I know no German, yet if a translation of a German poet had moved me, I would go to the British Museum and find books in English that would tell me something of his life, and of the history of his thought. But though these prose translations from Rabindranath Tagore have stirred my blood as nothing has for years, I shall not know anything of his life, and of the movements of thought that have made them possible, if some Indian traveller will not tell me." It seemed to him natural that I should be moved, for he said, "I read Rabindranath every day. To read one line of his is to forget all the troubles of the world." I said, "An Englishman living in London in the reign of Richard the Second, had he been shown translations from Petrarch or from Dante, would have found no books to answer his questions, but would have questioned some Florentine banker or Lombard merchant as I question you. For all I know, so abundant and simple is this poetry, the new Renaissance has been born in your country and

I shall never know of it except by hearsay." He answered, "We have other poets, but none that are his equal; we call this the epoch of Rabindranath. No poet seems to me as famous in Europe as he is among us. He is as great in music as in poetry, and his songs are sung from the west of India into Burma wherever Bengali is spoken. He was already famous at nineteen when he wrote his first novel; and plays, written when he was but little older, are still played in Calcutta. I so much admire the completeness of his life; when he was very young he wrote much of natural objects, he would sit all day in his garden; from his twenty-fifth year or so to his thirty-fifth perhaps, when he had a great sorrow, he wrote the most beautiful love poetry in our language"; and then he said with deep emotion, "words can never express what I owed at seventeen to his love poetry. After that his art grew deeper, it became religious and philosophical; all the aspirations of mankind are in his hymns. He is the first among our saints who has not refused to live, but has spoken out of Life itself, and that is why we give him our love." I may have changed his well-chosen words in my memory but not his thought. "A little while ago he was to read divine service in one of our churches — we of the Brahma Samaj use your word "church" in English — it was the largest in Calcutta and not only was it crowded, people even standing in the windows, but the streets were all but impassable because of the people."

Other Indians came to see me and their reverence for this man sounded strange in our world, where we hide great and little things under the same veil of obvious comedy and half-serious depreciation. When we were making the cathedrals had we a like reverence for our great men? "Every morning at three — I know, for I have seen it" — one said to me, "he sits immovable in contemplation, and for two hours does not awake from his reverie upon the nature of God. His father, the Maha Rishi, would sometimes sit there all through the next day; once, upon a river, he fell into contemplation because of the beauty of the landscape, and the rowers waited for eight hours before they could continue their journey." He then told me of Mr Tagore's family and how for generations great men have come out of its cradles. "Today," he said, "there are Gogonendranath and Abanindranath Tagore, who are artists; and Dwijendranath,

Rabindranath's brother, who is a great philosopher. The squirrels come from the boughs and climb on to his knees and the birds alight upon his hands." I notice in these men's thought a sense of visible beauty and meaning as though they held that doctrine of Nietzsche that we must not believe in the moral or intellectual beauty which does not sooner or later impress itself upon physical things. I said, "In the East you know how to keep a family illustrious. The other day the curator of a museum pointed out to me a little dark-skinned man who was arranging their Chinese prints and said, 'That is the hereditary connoisseur of the Mikado, he is the fourteenth of his family to hold the post.' He answered, "When Rabindranath was a boy he had all round him in his home literature and music." I thought of the abundance, of the simplicity of the poems, and said, "In your country is there much propagandist writing, much criticism? We have to do so much, especially in my own country, that our minds gradually cease to be creative, and yet we cannot help it. If our life was not a continual warfare, we would not have taste, we would not know what is good, we would not find hearers and readers. Four-fifths of our energy is spent in the quarrel with bad taste, whether in our own minds or in the minds of others." "I understand," he replied, "we too have our propagandist writing. In the villages they recite long mythological poems adapted from the Sanskrit in the Middle Ages, and they often insert passages telling the people that they must do their duties."

II

I have carried the manuscript of these translations about with me for days, reading it in railway trains, or on the top of omnibuses and in restaurants, and I have often had to close it lest some stranger would see how much it moved me. These lyrics — which are in the original, my Indians tell me, full of subtlety of rhythm, of untranslatable delicacies of colour, of metrical invention — display in their thought a world I have dreamed of all my life long. The work of a supreme culture, they yet appear as much the growth of the common soil as the grass and the rushes. A tradition, where poetry and religion are the same thing, has passed through the centuries, gathering from learned and unlearned metaphor and emotion, and carried back again to the multitude the thought of the scholar and of the noble. If the civilization of Bengal remains unbroken, if that common mind which — as one divines — runs through all, is not, as with us, broken into a dozen minds that know nothing of each other, something even of what is most subtle in these verses will have come, in a few generations, to the beggar on the roads. When there was but one mind in England, Chaucer wrote his *Troilus and Cressida,* and though he had written to be read, or to be read out — for our time was coming on apace — he was sung by minstrels for a while. Rabindranath Tagore, like Chaucer's forerunners, writes music for his words, and one understands at every moment that he is so abundant, so spontaneous, so daring in his passion, so full of surprise, because he is doing something which has never seemed strange, unnatural, or in need of defence. These verses will not lie in little well-printed books upon ladies' tables, who turn the pages with indolent hands that they may sigh over a life without meaning, which is yet all they can know of life, or be carried about by students at the university to be laid aside when the work of life begins, but, as the generations pass, travellers will hum them on the highway and men rowing upon rivers. Lovers, while they await one another, shall find, in murmuring them, this love of God a magic gulf wherein their own more bitter passion may bathe and renew its youth. At every moment the heart of this poet flows outward to these without derogation or condescension, for it has known that they will understand; and it has filled itself with the circumstance of their lives. The traveller in the red-brown clothes that he wears that dust may not show upon him, the girl searching in her bed for the petals fallen from the wreath of her royal lover, the servant or the bride awaiting the master's home-coming in the empty house, are images of the heart turning to God. Flowers and rivers, the blowing of conch shells, the heavy rain of the Indian July, or the parching heat, are images of the moods of that heart in union or in separation; and a man sitting in a boat upon a river playing upon a lute, like one of those figures full of mysterious meaning in a Chinese picture, is God Himself. A whole people, a whole civilization, immeasurably strange to us, seems to have been taken up into this imagination; and yet we are not moved because of its strangeness, but because we have met our own image, as though we had walked in Rossetti's willow wood, or heard, perhaps

11

for the first time in literature, our voice as in a dream.

Since the Renaissance the writing of European saints — however familiar their metaphor and the general structure of their thought — has ceased to hold our attention. We know that we must at last forsake the world, and we are accustomed in moments of weariness or exaltation to consider a voluntary forsaking; but how can we, who have read so much poetry, seen so many paintings, listened to so much music, where the cry of the flesh and the cry of the soul seem one, forsake it harshly and rudely? What have we in common with St Bernard covering his eyes that they may not dwell upon the beauty of the lakes of Switzerland, or with the violent rhetoric of the Book of Revelation? We would, if we might, find, as in this book, words full of courtesy. "I have got my leave. Bid me farewell, my brothers! I bow to you all and take my departure. Here I give back the keys of my door — and I give up all claims to my house. I only ask for last kind words from you. We were neighbours for long, but I received more than I could give. Now the day has dawned and the lamp that lit my dark corner is out. A summons has come and I am ready for my journey." And it is our own mood, when it is furthest from a Kempis or John of the Cross, that cries, "And because I love this life, I know I shall love death as well." Yet it is not only in our thoughts of the parting that this book fathoms all. We had not known that we loved God, hardly it may be that we believed in Him; yet looking backward upon our life we discover, in our exploration of the pathways of woods, in our delight in the lonely places of hills, in that mysterious claim that we have made, unavailingly, on the women that we have loved, the emotion that created this insidious sweetness. "Entering my heart unbidden even as one of the common crowd, unknown to me, my king, thou didst press the signet of eternity upon many a fleeting moment." This is no longer the sanctity of the cell and of the scourge; being but a lifting up, as it were, into a greater intensity of the mood of the painter, painting the dust and the sunlight, and we go for a like voice to St Francis and to William Blake who have seemed so alien in our violent history.

III

We write long books where no page

13

perhaps has any quality to make writing a pleasure, being confident in some general design, just as we fight and make money and fill our heads with politics — all dull things in the doing — while Mr Tagore, like the Indian civilization itself, has been content to discover the soul and surrender himself to its spontaneity. He often seems to contrast his life with that of those who have lived more after our fashion, and have more seeming weight in the world, and always humbly as though he were only sure his way is best for him: "Men going home glance at me and smile and fill me with shame. I sit like a begger maid, drawing my skirt over my face, and when they ask me, what it is I want, I drop my eyes and answer them not." At another time, remembering how his life had once a different shape, he will say, "Many an hour have I spent in the strife of the good and the evil, but now it is the pleasure of my playmate of the empty days to draw my heart on to him; and I know not why is this sudden call to what useless inconsequence." An innocence, a simplicity that one does not find elsewhere in literature makes the birds and the leaves seem as near to him as they are near to children, and the changes of the seasons great events as before our thoughts had arisen between them and us. At times I wonder if he has it from the literature of Bengal or from religion, and at other times, remembering the birds alighting on his brother's hands, I find pleasure in thinking it hereditary, a mystery that was growing through the centuries like the courtesy of a Tristan or a Pelanore. Indeed, when he is speaking of children, so much a part of himself this quality seems, one is not certain that he is not also speaking of the saints, "They build their houses with sand and they play with empty shells. With withered leaves they weave their boats and smilingly float them on the vast deep. Children have their play on the seashore of worlds. They know not how to swim, they know not how to cast nets. Pearl fishers dive for pearls, merchants sail in their ships, while children gather pebbles and scatter them again. They seek not for hidden treasures, they know not how to cast nets."

W.B. Yeats

1

God wants the human soul to live for ever, and renews human life constantly. God is a flute-player, playing ever new melodies on the flute that is the poet. It is God who inspires him to sing with ecstatic joy. God pours out His abundant gifts, but human beings are too small to use them fully.

THOU hast made me endless, such is thy pleasure. This frail vessel thou emptiest again and again, and fillest it ever with fresh life.

This little flute of a reed thou hast carried over hills and dales, and hast breathed through it melodies eternally new.

At the immortal touch of thy hands my little heart loses its limits in joy and gives birth to utterance ineffable.

Thy infinite gifts come to me only on these very small hands of mine. Ages pass, and still thou pourest, and still there is room to fill.

2

*The poet is enraptured. He is in communion
with his Maker whom he meets face to face.
Music purifies and ennobles the human soul and
elevates it to oneness with God. Only inspired
musicians can have this mystic experience of
friendship with Him.*

WHEN thou commandest me to sing it
seems that my heart would break with pride;
and I look to thy face, and tears come to
my eyes.

All that is harsh and dissonant in my
life melts into one sweet harmony — and
my adoration spreads wings like a glad bird
on its flight across the sea.

I know thou takest pleasure in my
singing. I know that only as a singer I come
before thy presence.

I touch by the edge of the far-spreading
wing of my song thy feet which I could never
aspire to reach.

Drunk with the joy of singing I forget
myself and call thee friend who art my lord.

3

God is the Supreme Musician whose music is the very creation. His music fills the universe with light and life and makes the poet aware that he is incapable and imperfect. Yet ceaseless music captivates him.

I KNOW not how thou singest, my master! I ever listen in silent amazement.

The light of thy music illumines the world. The life breath of thy music runs from sky to sky. The holy stream of thy music breaks through all stony obstacles and rushes on.

My heart longs to join in thy song, but vainly struggles for a voice. I would speak, but speech breaks not into song, and I cry out baffled. Ah, thou hast made my heart captive in the endless meshes of thy music, my master!

4

God is present everywhere. Man should keep his body, mind and heart pure and spotless, as a holy temple of God who is the source of life, truth, wisdom and love, and who dwells in him. His actions should manifest the greatness and glory of God.

LIFE of my life, I shall ever try to keep my body pure, knowing that thy living touch is upon all my limbs.

I shall ever try to keep all untruths out from my thoughts, knowing that thou art that truth which has kindled the light of reason in my mind.

I shall ever try to drive all evils away from my heart and keep my love in flower, knowing that thou hast thy seat in the inmost shrine of my heart.

And it shall be my endeavour to reveal thee in my actions, knowing it is thy power gives me strength to act.

5

The poet, fed up with worldly occupations, longs for a time of peaceful contemplation in the presence of God. Other matters could be taken care of later. All things in nature offer devotion to their Creator, and the contemplation of their beauty and harmony leads the poet to communion with Him.

I ASK for a moment's indulgence to sit by thy side. The works that I have in hand I will finish afterwards.

Away from the sight of thy face my heart knows no rest nor respite, and my work becomes an endless toil in a shoreless sea of toil.

Today the summer has come at my window with its sighs and murmurs; and the bees are plying their minstrelsy at the court of the flowering grove.

Now it is time to sit quiet, face to face with thee, and to sing dedication of life in this silent and overflowing leisure.

6

The poet humbly makes of his life a flower-offering to God. Though this flower, without deep colour or strong scent, is not worthy of the Master's head, it may still be placed on His feet.

PLUCK this little flower and take it, delay not! I fear lest it droop and drop into the dust.

It may not find a place in thy garland, but honour it with a touch of pain from thy hand and pluck it. I fear lest the day end before I am aware, and the time of offering go by.

Though its colour be not deep and its smell be faint, use this flower in thy service and pluck it while there is time.

7

Simplicity and honesty are essential for communion with the Divine while vanity and pride hinder perfect communion. The poet's vanity disappears when he meets God face to face. He can sing only when his life is simple and straightforward.

MY song has put off her adornments. She has no pride of dress and decoration. Ornaments would mar our union; they would come between thee and me; their jingling would drown thy whispers.

My poet's vanity dies in shame before thy sight. O master poet, I have sat down at thy feet. Only let me make my life simple and straight, like a flute of reed for thee to fill with music.

8

Material riches and earthly power are condemned. Luxurious dress and ornaments prevent solidarity and communion with the humble masses. The child who is dressed in costly clothes cannot play freely and enjoy himself lest he should soil them. Isolation from fellow beings causes spiritual ruin.

THE child who is decked with prince's robes and who has jewelled chains round his neck loses all pleasure in his play; his dress hampers him at every step.

In fear that it may be frayed, or stained with dust he keeps himself from the world, and is afraid even to move.

Mother, it is no gain, thy bondage of finery, if it keep one shut off from the healthful dust of the earth, if it rob one of the right of entrance to the great fair of common human life.

9

We should trustingly abandon ourselves in the hands of the wise and loving God. As He carries the burden of the whole universe, so will he carry the burden of our life, too. It is best for us to forget the past and to venture into the future with hope and courage.

O FOOL, to try to carry thyself upon thy own shoulders! O beggar, to come to beg at thy own door!

Leave all thy burdens on his hands who can bear all, and never look behind in regret.

Thy desire at once puts out the light from the lamp it touches with its breath. It is unholy — take not thy gifts through its unclean hands. Accept only what is offered by sacred love.

10

God loves the humble and lives among them.
Those who want to meet God should look for
Him among the poor and the lowly. Loving
service to them is the best form of worship of
God.

HERE is thy footstool and there rest thy feet
where live the poorest, and lowliest, and
lost.

When I try to bow to thee, my
obeisance cannot reach down to the depth
where thy feet rest among the poorest, and
lowliest, and lost.

Pride can never approach to where
thou walkest in the clothes of the humble
among the poorest, and lowliest, and lost.

My heart can never find its way to
where thou keepest company with the
companionless among the poorest, the
lowliest, and the lost.

11

Living in a secluded and unreal world, away from the toil and moil of humble humanity, is no way of meeting God. Without fraternal solidarity and universal brotherhood, devotional and ascetical practices are of no avail. Acceptance of reality, not its rejection, is the way to God-realisation.

LEAVE this chanting and singing and telling of beads! Whom dost thou worship in this lonely dark corner of a temple with doors all shut? Open thine eyes and see thy God is not before thee!

He is there where the tiller is tilling the hard ground and where the pathmaker is breaking stones. He is with them in sun and in shower, and his garment is covered with dust. Put off thy holy mantle and even like him come down on the dusty soil!

Deliverance? Where is this deliverance to be found? Our master himself has joyfully taken upon him the bonds of creation; he is bound with us all for ever.

Come out of thy meditations and leave aside thy flowers and incense! What harm is there if thy clothes become tattered and stained? Meet him and stand by him in toil and in sweat of thy brow.

12

*The human soul travels far and wide searching
for the Divine before he returns to his own self
and finds Him in the sanctuary of his own heart.
God is immanent as well as omnipresent.*

THE time that my journey takes is long and
the way of it long.

I came out on the chariot of the first
gleam of light, and pursued my voyage
through the wilderness of worlds leaving my
track on many a star and planet.

It is the most distant course that comes
nearest to thyself, and that training is the
most intricate which leads to the utter
simplicity of a tune.

The traveller has to knock at every alien
door to come to his own, and one has to
wander through all the outer worlds to reach
the innermost shrine at the end.

My eyes strayed far and wide before I
shut them and said "Here art thou!"

The question and the cry "Oh, where?"

melt into tears of a thousand streams and deluge the world with the flood of the assurance "I am!"

13

The poet is yearning to attain communion with the Divine, yet he is unable to fulfil this yearning. He does love God, but his love is far from perfect. Though he hears His footsteps, he fails to see His face, for he has still to grow in wisdom and purity of soul. Long and patient preparation and self-purification are necessary for communion with God.

THE song that I came to sing remains unsung to this day.

I have spent my days in stringing and in unstringing my instrument.

The tune has not come true, the words have not been rightly set; only there is the agony of wishing in my heart.

The blossom has not opened; only the wind is sighing by.

I have not seen his face, nor have I listened to his voice; only I have heard his gentle footsteps from the road before my house.

The livelong day has passed in spreading his seat on the floor; but the lamp has not been lit and I cannot ask him into my house.

I live in the hope of meeting with him; but this meeting is not yet.

14

*God is merciful, and therefore does not grant
the worldly desires of the poet, thus helping him
towards self-purification and enabling him to
enjoy His many and great gifts. The nobler and
purer man grows, the nearer to God he comes.*

MY desires are many and my cry is pitiful,
but ever didst thou save me by hard refusals;
and this strong mercy has been wrought into
my life through and through.

Day by day thou art making me worthy
of the simple, great gifts that thou gavest to
me unasked — this sky and the light, this
body and the life and the mind — saving
me from perils of overmuch desire.

There are times when I languidly linger
and times when I awaken and hurry in
search of my goal; but cruelly thou hidest
thyself from before me.

Day by day thou art making me worthy
of thy full acceptance by refusing me ever
and anon, saving me from perils of weak,
uncertain desire.

15

In God's great world, the poet is happy to be in his humble place. With his insignificant song-offering, he awaits the call of the merciful and loving God to sing.

I AM here to sing thee songs. In this hall of thine I have a corner seat.

In thy world I have no work to do; my useless life can only break out in tunes without a purpose.

When the hour strikes for thy silent worship at the dark temple of midnight, command me, my master, to stand before thee to sing.

When in the morning air the golden harp is tuned, honour me, commanding my presence.

16

God has spread out His abundant gifts and blessings in the grand festival of this world. The poet's part in this festival is to sing songs to his Maker. He does his best at it, but his longing is for re-union with the Infinite.

I HAVE had my invitation to this world's festival, and thus my life has been blessed. My eyes have seen and my ears have heard.

It was my part at this feast to play upon my instrument, and I have done all I could.

Now, I ask, has the time come at last when I may go in and see thy face and offer thee my silent salutation?

17

True love consists not in the observance of rules and customs, but in self-surrender. Therefore, ignoring the protests of the people, the poet abandons them, and, like a woman in love, awaits the coming of God, his Lover, to surrender himself to Him.

I AM only waiting for love to give myself up at last into his hands. That is why it is so late and why I have been guilty of such omissions.

They come with their laws and their codes to bind me fast; but I evade them ever, for I am only waiting for love to give myself up at last into his hands.

People blame me and call me heedless; I doubt not they are right in their blame.

The market day is over and work is all done for the busy. Those who came to call me vain have gone back in anger. I am only waiting for love to give myself up at last into his hands.

18

In the dark and cloudy night the poet keeps vigil at the door of God, his Lover, but He does not grant him entrance. So the poet feels lonely and lost, and his heart cries in sadness.

CLOUDS heap upon clouds and it darkens. Ah, love, why dost thou let me wait outside at the door all alone?

In the busy moments of the noontide work I am with the crowd, but on this dark lonely day it is only for thee that I hope.

If thou showest me not thy face, if thou leavest me wholly aside, I know not how I am to pass these long, rainy hours.

I keep gazing on the far-away gloom of the sky, and my heart wanders wailing with the restless wind.

19

God still does not respond to the poet's prayer, but he continues to wait for Him. As the night vigil will be rewarded with day-break, so his long waiting will be rewarded, and God will speak to him in the song of birds and in the beauty of wild flowers. This calls for self-purification, and the poet has decided to undergo that.

IF thou speakest not I will fill my heart with thy silence and endure it. I will keep still and wait like the night with starry vigil and its head bent low with patience.

The morning will surely come, the darkness will vanish, and thy voice pour down in golden streams breaking through the sky.

Then thy words will take wing in songs from every one of my birds' nests, and thy melodies will break forth in flowers in all my forest groves.

20

God dwells in our hearts, and it is there that we should find Him. Like the musk deer that wanders in pursuit of the fragrance not knowing the fragrance comes from itself, the poet wanders in vain without searching for God who dwells within.

ON the day when the lotus bloomed, alas, my mind was straying, and I knew it not. My basket was empty and the flower remained unheeded.

Only now and again a sadness fell upon me, and I started up from my dream and felt a sweet trace of a strange fragrance in the south wind.

That vague sweetness made my heart ache with longing and it seemed to me that it was the eager breath of the summer seeking for its completion.

I knew not then that it was so near, that it was mine, and that this perfect sweetness had blossomed in the depth of my own heart.

21

The spring flowers have disappeared and the autumn leaves are falling, yet the poet is still waiting for God, his Lover. But now the waves of the sea invite him and sweet music from the other shore urges him. The pull of the Eternal is irresistible.

I MUST launch out my boat. The languid hours pass by on the shore — Alas for me!

The spring has done its flowering and taken leave. And now with the burden of faded futile flowers I wait and linger.

The waves have become clamorous, and upon the bank in the shady lane the yellow leaves flutter and fall.

What emptiness do you gaze upon! Do you not feel a thrill passing through the air with the notes of the far-away song floating from the other shore?

22

Like a lover going in stealth to meet his sweetheart, the eternal Lover goes about in secret. The storm rages in deep darkness. The poet alone waits with open door for his divine Lover and invites Him to come in.

IN the deep shadows of the rainy July, with secret steps, thou walkest, silent as night, eluding all watchers.

Today the morning has closed its eyes, heedless of the insistent calls of the loud east wind, and a thick veil has been drawn over the ever-wakeful blue sky.

The woodlands have hushed their songs, and doors are all shut at every house. Thou art the solitary wayfarer in this deserted street. Oh my only friend, my best beloved, the gates are open in my house — do not pass by like a dream.

23

In the dark and stormy night the poet is still waiting anxiously for his Lover. From time to time he opens the door expecting the Lover, but He is not yet seen. But He is a fearless Lover who surely comes to His beloved who awaits Him.

ART thou abroad on this stormy night on thy journey of love, my friend? The sky groans like one in despair.

I have no sleep tonight. Ever and again I open my door and look out on the darkness, my friend!

I can see nothing before me. I wonder where lies thy path!

By what dim shore of the ink-black river, by what far edge of the frowning forest, through what mazy depth of gloom art thou threading thy course to come to me, my friend?

24

God in His mercy gives night and sleep to the tired creatures, so that they wake up restored and renewed the next morning. The poet, tired and without provisions, prays for renewal of his strength, and welcomes death through which he would be reborn into new life.

IF the day is done, if birds sing no more, if the wind has flagged tired, then draw the veil of darkness thick upon me, even as thou hast wrapt the earth with the coverlet of sleep and tenderly closed the petals of the drooping lotus at dusk.

From the traveller, whose sack of provisions is empty before the voyage is ended, whose garment is torn and dustladen, whose strength is exhausted, remove shame and poverty, and renew his life like a flower under the cover of thy kindly night.

25

By absolute faith in God and total surrender of oneself to Him, one prepares for God-realisation. The poet, exhausted, will go to sleep with full faith in God and in surrender to Him. He is confident of coming to new life through death.

IN the night of weariness let me give myself up to sleep without struggle, resting my trust upon thee.

Let me not force my flagging spirit into a poor preparation for thy worship.

It is thou who drawest the veil of night upon the tired eyes of the day to renew its sight in a fresher gladness of awakening.

26

The Divine Lover comes quietly, but the poet is asleep in the night of his ignorance and material preoccupations. Thus he misses the opportunity and then feels sorry about it.

HE came and sat by my side but I woke not. What a cursed sleep it was, O miserable me!

He came when the night was still; he had his harp in his hands, and my dreams became resonant with its melodies.

Alas, why are my nights all thus lost? Ah, why do I ever miss his sight whose breath touches my sleep?

27

*In the rainy dark night the ever wakeful Divine
Lover calls the poet, His beloved, to come out
and meet Him, but the latter fails to find his way,
for his love is no more than momentary flashes.
All darkness and difficulties will be overcome
by the devotee if his heart is inflamed with love.*

LIGHT, oh where is the light? Kindle it with
the burning fire of desire!

There is the lamp but never a flicker of
a flame — is such thy fate, my heart? Ah,
death were better by far for thee!

Misery knocks at thy door, and her
message is that thy lord is wakeful, and he
calls thee to the love-tryst through the
darkness of night.

The sky is overcast with clouds and the
rain is ceaseless. I know not what this is that
stirs in me — I know not its meaning.

A moment's flash of lightning drags
down a deeper gloom on my sight, and my
heart gropes for the path to where the music
of the night calls me.

Light, oh where is the light! Kindle it with the burning fire of desire! It thunders and the wind rushes screaming through the void. The night is black as a black stone. Let not the hours pass by in the dark. Kindle the lamp of love with thy life.

28

The poet is torn between two loves. He longs for communion with the Divine, yet is afraid to renounce the world.

OBSTINATE are the trammels, but my heart aches when I try to break them.

Freedom is all I want, but to hope for it I feel ashamed.

I am certain that priceless wealth is in thee, and that thou art my best friend, but I have not the heart to sweep away the tinsel that fills my room.

The shroud that covers me is a shroud of dust and death; I hate it, yet hug it in love.

My debts are large, my failures great, my shame secret and heavy; yet when I come to ask for my good, I quake in fear lest my prayer be granted.

29

The human soul is imprisoned by pride and power. The more he cares for material possessions, the more forgetful man becomes of his spiritual reality. Tagore condemns avarice, not the wholesome pleasures of life.

HE whom I enclose with my name is weeping in this dungeon. I am ever busy building this wall all around; and as this wall goes up into the sky day by day I lose sight of my true being in its dark shadow.

I take pride in this great wall, and I plaster it with dust and sand lest a least hole should be left in this name; and for all the care I take I lose sight of my true being.

30

As the poet goes to meet his Lover and Master, he is pursued and troubled by his own ego and vainglory. Spiritual progress requires that we give up our egocentrism.

I CAME out alone on my way to my tryst. But who is this that follows me in the silent dark?

I move aside to avoid his presence but I escape him not.

He makes the dust rise from the earth with his swagger; he adds his loud voice to every word that I utter.

He is my own little self, my lord, he knows no shame; but I am ashamed to come to thy door in his company.

*Man uses his power and pelf for his own
pleasure, and thus becomes their captive. Only
a charitable use of wealth can bring one spiritual
freedom. "It is much harder for a rich person to
enter the Kingdom of God than for a camel to
go through the eye of a needle" (Mk 10:25).*

"PRISONER, tell me, who was it that bound
you?"

"It was my master," said the prisoner.
"I thought I could outdo everybody in the
world in wealth and power, and I amassed
in my own treasure-house the money due
to my king. When sleep overcame me I lay
upon the bed that was for my lord, and on
waking up I found I was a prisoner in my
own treasure-house."

"Prisoner, tell me, who was it that
wrought this unbreakable chain?"

"It was I," said the prisoner, "who
forged this chain very carefully. I thought
my invincible power would hold the world
captive leaving me in a freedom

undisturbed. Thus night and day I worked at the chain with huge fires and cruel hard strokes. When at last the work was done and the links were complete and unbreakable, I found that it held me in its grip."

32

Genuine love is self-sacrificing and desires the good of the other. Unlike worldly lovers, God is not possessive; He allows full freedom in love. Even if man forgets Him, God remains constant in His love.

BY all means they try to hold me secure who love me in this world. But it is otherwise with thy love which is greater than theirs, and thou keepest me free.

Lest I forget them they never venture to leave me alone. But day passes by after day and thou art not seen.

If I call not thee in my prayers, if I keep not thee in my heart, thy love for me still waits for my love.

33

Earthly desires subdue the human soul and gradually take it away from God. Unholy desires and love for wealth enter the soul like dishonest guests and rob the soul of all that is spiritual.

WHEN it was day they came into my house and said, "We shall only take the smallest room here."

They said, "We shall help you in the worship of your God and humbly accept only our own share of his grace"; and then they took their seat in a corner and they sat quiet and meek.

But in the darkness of night I find they break into my sacred shrine, strong and turbulent, and snatch with unholy greed the offerings from God's altar.

34

Tagore prays that his pride and vanity and all that is wicked in him may be destroyed and only that part of him which is spiritual and loves God be spared so that he may see God always and in all things.

LET only that little be left of me whereby I may name thee my all.

Let only that little be left of my will whereby I may feel thee on every side, and come to thee in everything, and offer to thee my love every moment.

Let only that little be left of me whereby I may never hide thee.

Let only that little of my fetters be left whereby I am bound with thy will, and thy purpose is carried out in my life — and that is the fetter of thy love.

35

This is a prayer for spiritual emancipation, true freedom and the fullness of life. The poet prays that his countrymen may be broadminded and live a fearless and noble life, with no divisions among them.

WHERE the mind is without fear and the head is held high;

Where knowledge is free;

Where the world has not been broken up into fragments by narrow domestic walls;

Where words come out from the depth of truth;

Where tireless striving stretches its arms towards perfection;

Where the clear stream of reason has not lost its way into the dreary desert sand of dead habit;

Where the mind is led forward by thee into ever-widening thought and action—

Into that heaven of freedom, my Father, let my country awake.

36

The poet prays his Maker for liberation from spiritual poverty and for strength to bear joys and sorrows with equanimity, to offer loving service to others, to stand up to the powerful and the proud, to befriend the poor, and always to surrender himself to His will.

THIS is my prayer to thee, my lord — strike, strike at the root of penury in my heart.

Give me the strength lightly to bear my joys and sorrows.

Give me the strength to make my love fruitful in service.

Give me the strength never to disown the poor or bend my knees before insolent might.

Give me the strength to raise my mind high above daily trifles.

And give me the strength to surrender my strength to thy will with love.

37

The traveller is tired and finds himself in a blind alley, with his provisions exhausted. He hopes for quiet rest, but God urges him and he moves ahead. The poet feels exhausted and blocked, but divine grace inspires him with new melodies and a new vision.

I THOUGHT that my voyage had come to its end at the last limit of my power, — that the path before me was closed, that provisions were exhausted and the time come to take shelter in a silent obscurity.

But I find that thy will knows no end in me. And when old words die out on the tongue, new melodies break forth from the heart; and where the old tracks are lost, new country is revealed with its wonders.

38

The poet is confused by his own many desires. But the only real and constant desire is for reunion with his Creator. In spite of darkness and momentary storms in his heart, the longing for communion with the Divine prevails.

THAT I want thee, only thee — let my heart repeat without end. All desires that distract me, day and night, are false and empty to the core.

As the night keeps hidden in its gloom the petition for light, even thus in the depth of my unconsciousness rings the cry — "I want thee, only thee."

As the storm still seeks its end in peace when it strikes against peace with all its might, even thus my rebellion strikes against thy love and still its cry is — "I want thee, only thee."

39

The poet continues his prayer, asking God to shower His mercy upon him when the love in his heart is dried up, to grant him beauty and sweet melody when he is deprived of them, to bring him peace and repose when he is bewildered and perplexed, to give him courage when he is frightened, to bring him back to the right path when he is misguided by worldly desires.

WHEN the heart is hard and parched up, come upon me with a shower of mercy.

When grace is lost from life, come with a burst of song.

When tumultuous work raises its din on all sides shutting me out from beyond, come to me, my lord of silence, with thy peace and rest.

When my beggarly heart sits crouched, shut up in a corner, break open the door, my king, and come with the ceremony of a king.

When desire blinds the mind with

delusion and dust, O thou holy one, thou wakeful, come with thy light and thy thunder.

40

The poet experiences spiritual aridity and longs for showers of divine blessing, but the showers do not come. This seeming indifference of God pains the poet deeply. He would rather welcome God's punishment, for he knows that He will grant him mercy thereafter.

THE rain has held back for days and days, my God, in my arid heart. The horizon is fiercely naked — not the thinnest cover of a soft cloud, not the vaguest hint of a distant cool shower.

Send thy angry storm, dark with death, if it is thy wish, and with lashes of lightning startle the sky from end to end.

But call back, my lord, call back this pervading silent heat, still and keen and cruel, burning the heart with dire despair.

Let the cloud of grace bend low from above like the tearful look of the mother on the day of the father's wrath.

41

*Here the poet portrays himself as a flower-girl,
the beloved of God. She waits long and in vain
for her Lover. Others come and take away her
flowers of love. The passers-by make fun of her.
But in silence she awaits her Lover, with longing,
sweet dreams and tears.*

WHERE dost thou stand behind them all,
my lover, hiding thyself in the shadows?
They push thee and pass thee by on the
dusty road, taking thee for naught. I wait
here weary hours spreading my offerings
for thee, while passers-by come and take
my flowers, one by one, and my basket is
nearly empty.

The morning time is past, and the
noon. In the shade of evening my eyes are
drowsy with sleep. Men going home glance
at me and smile and fill me with shame. I
sit like a beggar maid, drawing my skirt over
my face, and when they ask me, what it is I
want, I drop my eyes and answer them not.

Oh, how, indeed, could I tell them that

for thee I wait, and that thou hast promised to come. How could I utter for shame that I keep for my dowry this poverty. Ah, I hug this pride in the secret of my heart.

I sit on the grass and gaze upon the sky and dream of the sudden splendour of thy coming — all the lights ablaze, golden pennons flying over thy car, and they at the roadside standing agape, when they see thee come down from thy seat to raise me from the dust, and set at thy side this ragged beggar girl a-tremble with shame and pride, like a creeper in a summer breeze.

But time glides on and still no sound of the wheels of thy chariot. Many a procession passes by with noise and shouts and glamour of glory. Is it only thou who wouldst stand in the shadow silent and behind them all? And only I who would wait and weep and wear out my heart in vain longing?

42

In early life the poet felt persuaded that the Divine Master would come and take him across the ocean of eternity. Under His inspiration he would sing new and sweet melodies. But the Master does not come, and the poet is disappointed. He longs for rest and liberation from this world.

EARLY in the day it was whispered that we should sail in a boat, only thou and I, and never a soul in the world would know of this our pilgrimage to no country and to no end.

In that shoreless ocean, at thy silently listening smile my songs would swell in molodies, free as waves, free from all bondage of words.

Is the time not come yet? Are there works still to do? Lo, the evening has come down upon the shore and in the fading light the seabirds come flying to their nests.

Who knows when the chains will be off, and the boat, like the last glimmer of sunset, vanish into the night?

43

God the Supreme Master of all things is omnipresent. He enters our hearts unnoticed and influences our actions; so we need to be ever ready. God is present in the humblest of his creatures as well as in the great heavens.

THE day was when I did not keep myself in readiness for thee; and entering my heart unbidden even as one of the common crowd, unknown to me, my king, thou didst press the signet of eternity upon many a fleeting moment of my life.

And today when by chance I light upon them and see thy signature, I find they have lain scattered in the dust mixed with the memory of joys and sorrows of my trivial days forgotten.

Thou didst not turn in contempt from my childish play among dust, and the steps that I heard in my playroom are the same that are echoing from star to star.

44

Day and night, summer and rainy season, the poet awaits his divine Lover. Light, rain and haze bring His messages and greetings. The fragrance of the Lover fills the air, announcing His approach, and the poet sings with joy.

THIS is my delight, thus to wait and watch at the wayside where shadow chases light and the rain comes in the wake of the summer.

Messengers, with tidings from unknown skies, greet me and speed along the road. My heart is glad within, and the breath of the passing breeze is sweet.

From dawn till dusk I sit here before my door, and I know that of a sudden the happy moment will arrive when I shall see.

In the meanwhile I smile and I sing all alone. In the meanwhile the air is filling with the perfume of promise.

45

God ever comes to us silently, intently and endlessly, in forms of spring and fragrance, cloud and rain. He is present in nature and in the life of people. He inspires the poet with song, and His visit cheers him in moments of grief.

HAVE you not heard his silent steps? He comes, comes, ever comes.

Every moment and every age, every day and every night he comes, comes, ever comes.

Many a song have I sung in many a mood of mind, but all their notes have always proclaimed, "He comes, comes, ever comes."

In the fragrant days of sunny April through the forest path he comes, comes, ever comes.

In the rainy gloom of July nights on the thundering chariot of clouds he comes, comes, ever comes.

In sorrow after sorrow it is his steps that press upon my heart, and it is the golden touch of his feet that makes my joy to shine.

46

God is present in the bright bodies of heaven, yet he stays close to the poet who, like any true devotee, can see God who dwells in him. The poet hears His footsteps and must now leave all his activities and get ready to welcome Him.

I KNOW not from what distant time thou art ever coming nearer to meet me. Thy sun and stars can never keep thee hidden from me for aye.

In many a morning and eve thy footsteps have been heard and thy messenger has come within my heart and called me in secret.

I know not why today my life is all astir, and a feeling of tremulous joy is passing through my heart.

It is as if the time were come to wind up my work, and I feel in the air a faint smell of thy sweet presence.

47

The Divine Lover is delayed in coming. The poet is wearied; he is afraid he would be asleep when the Lover comes. He does not want to be awakened by the attractions and delights of the world, but only by the touch of the Divine Lover. The poet anticipates the bliss of seeing God face to face.

THE night is nearly spent waiting for him in vain. I fear lest in the morning he suddenly come to my door when I have fallen asleep wearied out. Oh friends, leave the way open to him — forbid him not.

If the sound of his steps does not wake me, do not try to rouse me, I pray. I wish not to be called from my sleep by the clamorous choir of birds, by the riot of wind at the festival of morning light. Let me sleep undisturbed even if my lord comes of a sudden to my door.

Ah, my sleep, precious sleep, which only waits for his touch to vanish. Ah, my closed eyes that would open their lids only to the light of his smile when he stands before me like a dream emerging from darkness of sleep.

Let him appear before my sight as the first of all lights and all forms. The first thrill of joy to my awakened soul let it come from his glance. And let my return to myself be immediate return to him.

48

People are too busy to worship God or to appreciate His glory manifested in nature. The poet and companions set out on the journey, neither resting nor stopping nor caring for nature's beauty. As the heat of the sun increased, the poet lay down to rest. His companions mocked him and moved on. He slept and woke up and saw the Divine standing before him. Not our wilful effort but total surrender to His will is the way to God-realisation.

THE morning sea of silence broke into ripples of bird songs; and the flowers were all merry by the roadside; and the wealth of gold was scattered through the rift of the clouds while we busily went on our way and paid no heed.

We sang no glad songs nor played; we went not to the village for barter; we spoke not a word nor smiled; we lingered not on the way. We quickened our pace more and more as the time sped by.

The sun rose to the mid sky and doves

cooed in the shade. Withered leaves danced and whirled in the hot air of noon. The shepherd boy drowsed and dreamed in the shadow of the banyan tree, and I laid myself down by the water and stretched my tired limbs on the grass.

My companions laughed at me in scorn; they held their heads high and hurried on; they never looked back nor rested; they vanished in the distant blue haze. They crossed many meadows and hills, and passed through strange, far-away countries. All honour to you, heroic host of the interminable path! Mockery and reproach pricked me to rise, but found no response in me. I gave myself up for lost in the depth of a glad humiliation — in the shadow of a dim delight.

The repose of the sun-embroidered green gloom slowly spread over my heart. I forgot for what I had travelled, and I surrendered my mind without struggle to the maze of shadows and songs.

At last, when I woke from my slumber

and opened my eyes, I saw thee standing by me, flooding my sleep with thy smile. How I had feared that the path was long and wearisome, and the struggle to reach thee was hard!

49

Many maestros sing to God the great King in his Kingdom, but attracted by the poet's humble song, He comes down to his cottage and offers him a flower as a prize. God loves the humble and comes to them.

YOU came down from your throne and stood at my cottage door.

I was singing all alone in a corner, and the melody caught your ear. You came down and stood at my cottage door.

Masters are many in your hall, and songs are sung there at all hours. But the simple carol of this novice struck at your love. One plaintive little strain mingled with the great music of the world, and with a flower for a prize you came down and stopped at my cottage door.

50

The poet pictures himself as a beggar going from door to door. Unexpectedly God the great King appears to him in His glory. The beggar expects alms from the King; instead, to his bewilderment He asks him, "What have you to give to me?" He gives Him a single grain of corn from his bag. At the end of the day he discovers a little grain of gold in what he had collected and weeps for not having given all to God. One is reminded of what Jesus said: "The measure you give will be the measure you get back" (Lk 6:38).

I HAD gone a-begging from door to door in the village path, when thy golden chariot appeared in the distance like a gorgeous dream and I wondered who was this King of all kings!

My hopes rose high and methought my evil days were at an end, and I stood waiting for alms to be given unasked and for wealth scattered on all sides in the dust.

The chariot stopped where I stood. Thy glance fell on me and thou camest down with a smile. I felt that the luck of my life had come at last. Then of a sudden thou didst hold out thy right hand and say, "What hast thou to give to me?"

Ah, what a kingly jest was it to open thy palm to a beggar to beg! I was confused and stood undecided, and then from my wallet I slowly took out the least little grain of corn and gave it to thee.

But how great my surprise when at the day's end I emptied my bag on the floor to find a least little grain of gold among the poor heap. I bitterly wept and wished that I had had the heart to give thee my all.

51

God is presented here as the King for whom the villagers waited late into the night. Finally when He did come, they had closed the doors and retired. They heard knocks at their doors and the roar of chariot, but dismissed them as wind and thunder. When they were forced to get up, they found themselves unprepared; so they welcomed the King with empty hands and tattered carpets. Man needs to be constantly watchful for God's coming, and He expects no pompous welcome but only love and humility.

THE night darkened. Our day's works had been done. We thought that the last guest had arrived for the night and the doors in the village were all shut. Only some said the king was to come. We laughed and said "No, it cannot be!"

It seemed there were knocks at the door and we said it was nothing but the wind. We put out the lamps and lay down to sleep. Only some said, "It is the messenger!" we laughed and said "No, it must be the wind!"

There came a sound in the dead of the night. We sleepily thought it was the distant thunder. The earth shook, the walls rocked, and it troubled us in our sleep. Only some said it was the sound of wheels. We said in a drowsy murmur, "No, it must be the rumbling of clouds!"

The night was still dark when the drum sounded. The voice came "Wake up! Delay not!" we pressed our hands on our hearts and shuddered with fear. Some said, "Lo, there is the king's flag!" We stood up on our feet and cried "There is no time for delay!"

The king has come — but where are lights, where are wreaths? Where is the throne to seat him? Oh, shame! Oh utter shame! Where is the hall, the decorations? Someone has said, "Vain is this cry! Greet him with empty hands, lead him into thy rooms all bare!"

Open the doors, let the conch-shells be sounded! In the depth of the night has come the king of our dark, dreary house. The thunder roars in the sky. The darkness shudders with lightning. Bring out thy tattered piece of mat and spread it in the courtyard. With the storm has come of a sudden our king of the fearful night.

52

The Lover visits the beloved in the night; after He has left, the beloved searches for some gift left by the Lover, and finds no flower or spices or flower-vase which are symbols of earthly comforts and luxury, but finds the Lover's sword, sign of strength and fortitude in fighting evil within and without.

I THOUGHT I should ask of thee — but I dared not — the rose wreath thou hadst on thy neck. Thus I waited for the morning, when thou didst depart, to find a few fragments on the bed. And like a beggar I searched in the dawn only for a stray petal or two.

Ah me, what is it I find? What token left of thy love? It is no flower, no spices, no vase of perfumed water. It is thy mighty sword, flashing as a flame, heavy as a bolt of thunder. The young light of morning comes through the window and spreads itself upon thy bed. The morning bird twitters and asks, "Woman, what hast thou got?" No, it is no flower, nor spices, nor vase of perfumed water — it is thy dreadful sword.

I sit and muse in wonder, what gift is this of thine. I can find no place where to hide it. I am ashamed to wear it, frail as I am, and it hurts me when I press it to my bosom. Yet shall I bear in my heart this honour of the burden of pain, this gift of thine.

From now there shall be no fear left for me in this world, and thou shalt be victorious in all my strife. Thou hast left death for my companion and I shall crown him with my life. Thy sword is with me to cut asunder my bonds, and there shall be no fear left for me in the world.

From now I leave off all petty decorations. Lord of my heart, no more shall there be for me waiting and weeping in corners, no more coyness and sweetness of demeanour. Thou hast given me thy sword for adornment. No more doll's decorations for me!

53

The beauty of nature, symbolised by God's star-studded bracelet, is God's gift to us. Even more beautiful is His sword, so fascinating, yet so terrible. The poet presents here the beauty, love and mercy of God on the one hand, and His justice and punishment on the other.

BEAUTIFUL is thy wristlet, decked with stars and cunningly wrought in myriad-coloured jewels. But more beautiful to me thy sword with its curve of lightning like the outspread wings of the divine bird of Vishnu, perfectly poised in the angry red light of the sunset.

It quivers like the one last response of life in ecstasy of pain at the final stroke of death; it shines like the pure flame of being burning up earthly sense with one fierce flash.

Beautiful is thy wristlet, decked with starry gems; but thy sword, O lord of thunder, is wrought with uttermost beauty, terrible to behold or to think of.

54

Here the poet is a woman who goes with other women to fetch water from the village well. Others go away; she lingers. The Lover comes as a thirsty traveller. She offers him water. As He drinks, the whole atmosphere is transformed and uplifted. The poet's little act of charity and devotion is rewarded with divine bliss.

I ASKED nothing from thee; I uttered not my name to thine ear. When thou took'st thy leave I stood silent. I was alone by the well where the shadow of the tree fell aslant, and the women had gone home with their brown earthen pitchers full to the brim. They called me and shouted, "Come with us, the morning is wearing on to noon." But I languidly lingered awhile lost in the midst of vague musings.

I heard not thy steps as thou camest. Thine eyes were sad when they fell on me; thy voice was tired as thou spokest low — "Ah, I am a thirsty traveller." I started up from my day-dreams and poured water from my jar on thy joined palms. The leaves rustled overhead; the cuckoo sang from the unseen dark, and perfume of *babla* flowers came from the bend of the road.

I stood speechless with shame when my name thou didst ask. Indeed, what had I done for thee to keep me in remembrance? But the memory that I could give water to thee to allay thy thirst will cling to my heart and enfold it in sweetness. The morning hour is late, the bird sings in weary notes, *neem* leaves rustle overhead and I sit and think and think.

55

*The beloved stays at home idle while the Lover
sits alone at the end of the rugged path, bearing
the heat. A friend urges the beloved to hasten
despite the heat. As he goes out to meet the
Lover, sweet music will break forth from the very
path. Union with the Divine is demanding, but
at the same time blissful.*

LANGUOR is upon your heart and the slumber is still on your eyes.

Has not the word come to you that the flower is reigning in splendour among thorns? Wake, oh awaken! Let not the time pass in vain!

At the end of the stony path, in the country of virgin solitude, my friend is sitting all alone. Deceive him not. Wake, oh awaken!

What if the sky pants and trembles with the heat of the midday sun — what if the burning sand spreads its mantle of thirst —

Is there no joy in the deep of your heart? At every footfall of yours, will not the harp of the road break out in sweet music of pain?

56

As man needs God's love, He needs man's love, too. And so He delights in creating beautiful forms of life and gives man the experience of His presence. The beauty of nature is God's decoration to win man's love. Such union of divine and human love is the perfect form of love which God and man long for.

THUS it is that thy joy in me is so full. Thus it is that thou hast come down to me. O thou lord of all heavens, where would be thy love if I were not?

Thou hast taken me as thy partner of all this wealth. In my heart is the endless play of thy delight. In my life thy will is ever taking shape.

And for this, thou who art the King of kings hast decked thyself in beauty to captivate my heart. And for this thy love loses itself in the love of thy lover, and there art thou seen in the perfect union of two.

57

Light symbolises God's delight in the act of creation. Light is beautiful and pleasing. Divine light enlightens every person. Flowers blooming and butterflies dancing at the break of light are symbols of God's joy in creation. The joy of heaven overflows into the earth and floods it.

LIGHT, my light, the world-filling light, the eye-kissing light, heart-sweetening light!

Ah, the light dances, my darling, at the centre of my life; the light strikes, my darling, the chords of my love; the sky opens, the wind runs wild, laughter passes over the earth.

The butterflies spread their sails on the sea of light. Lilies and jasmines surge up on the crest of the waves of light.

The light is shattered into gold on every cloud, my darling, and it scatters gems in profusion.

Mirth spreads from leaf to leaf, my darling, and gladness without measure. The heaven's river has drowned its banks and the flood of joy is abroad.

58

Joy flows like a river and produces the rich growth of grass over the earth. God delights in creation and destruction, the latter being a renewal of life. The violent storm merrily uproots trees and shakes the earth. The joyful cycle of birth, death, destruction and renewal goes on.

LET all the strains of joy mingle in my last song — the joy that makes the earth flow over in the riotous excess of the grass, the joy that sets the twin brothers, life and death, dancing over the wide world, the joy that sweeps in with the tempest, shaking and waking all life with laughter, the joy that sits still with its tears on the open red lotus of pain, and the joy that throws everything it has upon the dust, and knows not a word.

59

God expresses His love and glory through His beautiful creation. The poet is thankful to God for the joys granted to him. Daybreak fills him with love and joy as it is the rebirth of light that had died in the night, and he glorifies God.

YES, I know, this is nothing but thy love, O beloved of my heart — this golden light that dances upon the leaves, these idle clouds sailing across the sky, this passing breeze leaving its coolness upon my forehead.

The morning light has flooded my eyes — this is thy message to my heart. Thy face is bent from above, thy eyes look down on my eyes, and my heart has touched thy feet.

60

Simple, innocent and carefree children play everywhere, no matter what the weather is; they play even in the next world. They are not concerned with material gains, but delight in building houses of sand, in blowing shells and in sailing boats of fallen leaves. Grown-ups too should learn to be like children in their detachment and surrender to God's will.

ON the seashore of endless worlds children meet. The infinite sky is motionless overhead and the restless water is boisterous. On the seashore of endless worlds the children meet with shouts and dances.

They build their houses with sand and they play with empty shells. With withered leaves they weave their boats and smilingly float them on the vast deep. Children have their play on the seashore of worlds.

They know not how to swim, they know not how to cast nets. Pearl fishers dive for pearls, merchants sail in their ships, while children gather pebbles and scatter them again. They seek not for hidden treasures, they know not how to cast nets.

The sea surges up with laughter and pale gleams the smile of the sea beach. Death-dealing waves sing meaningless ballads to the children, even like a mother while rocking her baby's cradle. The sea plays with children, and pale gleams the smile of the sea beach.

On the seashore of endless worlds children meet. Tempest roams in the pathless sky, ships get wrecked in the trackless water, death is abroad and children play. On the seashore of endless worlds is the great meeting of children.

61

*A baby is innocent and beautiful. His sleep is a
magic sleep; his smile is like the golden rays of
the dawn. His soft and beautiful limbs come from
the tender and loving heart of his mother.*

THE sleep that flits on baby's eyes — does
anybody know from where it comes? Yes,
there is a rumour that it has its dwelling
where, in the fairy village among shadows
of the forest dimly lit with glow-worms, there
hang two timid buds of enchantment. From
there it comes to kiss baby's eyes.

The smile that flickers on baby's lips
when he sleeps — does anybody know
where it was born? Yes, there is a rumour
that a young pale beam of a crescent moon
touched the edge of a vanishing autumn
cloud, and there the smile was first born in
the dream of a dew-washed morning — the
smile that flickers on baby's lips when he
sleeps.

The sweet, soft freshness that blooms
on baby's limbs — does anybody know

where it was hidden so long? Yes, when the mother was a young girl it lay pervading her heart in tender and silent mystery of love — the sweet, soft freshness that has bloomed on baby's limbs.

62

The parent loves the child deeply and fondles him with toys, sweets, songs and kisses. Similarly God has created colourful, sweet, bright and pleasant things to entertain all of us His children. The happiness of His children is His pleasure.

WHEN I bring to you coloured toys, my child, I understand why there is such a play of colours on clouds, on water, and why flowers are painted in tints — when I give coloured toys to you, my child.

When I sing to make you dance I truly know why there is music in leaves, and why waves send their chorus of voices to the heart of the listening earth — when I sing to make you dance.

When I bring sweet things to your greedy hands I know why there is honey in the cup of the flower and why fruits are secretly filled with sweet juice — when I bring sweet things to your greedy hands.

When I kiss your face to make you

smile, my darling, I surely understand what pleasure streams from the sky in morning light, and what delight that is which the summer breeze brings to my body — when I kiss you to make you smile.

63

*All things and all forms of life express the Divine.
All are friends and brothers, for all manifest the
one God. Death frightens us, for it is our passage
into the unfamiliar world, but God is our
companion everywhere. He takes pleasure in
constantly renewing the old. Man will no more
be afraid when he understands that all forms of
life manifest the Divine.*

THOU hast made me known to friends whom I knew not. Thou hast given me seats in homes not my own. Thou hast brought the distant near and made a brother of the stranger.

I am uneasy at heart when I have to leave my accustomed shelter; I forget that there abides the old in the new, and that there also thou abidest.

Through birth and death, in this world or in others, wherever thou leadest me it is thou, the same, the one companion of my endless life who ever linkest my heart with bonds of joy to the unfamiliar.

When one knows thee, then alien there is none, then no door is shut. Oh, grant me my prayer that I may never lose the bliss of the touch of the one in the play of the many.

64

It is not in rituals but in helping the suffering that true devotion to God consists. People waste their wealth on useless rituals and ignore the needy. Their devotion is indeed empty.

ON the slope of the desolate river among tall grasses I asked her, "Maiden, where do you go shading your lamp with your mantle? My house is all dark and lonesome — lend me your light!" She raised her dark eyes for a moment and looked at my face through the dusk. "I have come to the river," she said, "to float my lamp on the stream when the daylight wanes in the west." I stood alone among tall grasses and watched the timid flame of her lamp uselessly drifting in the tide.

In the silence of gathering night I asked her, "Maiden, your lights are all lit — then where do you go with your lamp? My house is all dark and lonesome — lend me your light." She raised her dark eyes on my face and stood for a moment doubtful. "I have come," she said at last, "to dedicate my lamp to the sky." I stood and watched her light uselessly burning in the void.

In the moonless gloom of midnight I asked her, "Maiden, what is your quest, holding the lamp near your heart? My house is all dark and lonesome — lend me your light." She stopped for a minute and thought and gazed at my face in the dark. "I have brought my light," she said, "to join the carnival of lamps." I stood and watched her little lamp uselessly lost among lights.

65

*Only under divine inspiration does the poet
write. Man is eternally related to God through
his devotion which brings joy to man and God
alike. God drinks the nectar of love from the
cup of human life; He plays sweet music on the
instrument that is man. Every noble
achievement, every mystic bliss, results from the
communion of God and man.*

WHAT divine drink wouldst thou have, my God, from this overflowing cup of my life?

My poet, is it thy delight to see thy creation through my eyes and to stand at the portals of my ears silently to listen to thine own eternal harmony?

Thy world is weaving words in my mind and thy joy is adding music to them. Thou givest thyself to me in love and then feelest thine own entire sweetness in me.

66

The poet hides in his heart the song which he wants to offer to His Maker as his last gift. This song is like a virgin who will show her face only to her husband. It has ever remained with the poet, ruling his heart and soul, yet ever secluded.

SHE who ever had remained in the depth of my being, in the twilight of gleams and of glimpses; she who never opened her veils in the morning light, will be my last gift to thee, my God, folded in my final song.

Words have wooed yet failed to win her; persuasion has stretched to her its eager arms in vain.

I have roamed from country to country keeping her in the core of my heart, and around her have risen and fallen the growth and decay of my life.

Over my thoughts and actions, my slumbers and dreams, she reigned yet dwelled alone and apart.

Many a man knocked at my door and asked for her and turned away in despair.

There was none in the world who ever saw her face to face, and she remained in her loneliness waiting for thy recognition.

67

God is infinite and at the same time finite. The human soul grows and matures in the divine soul which is its shelter. God manifests His beauty in innumerable things, in sunrise and in sunset. The boundless sky with its radiant light shows forth His infinite glory.

THOU art the sky and thou art the nest as well.

O thou beautiful, there in the nest it is thy love that encloses the soul with colours and sounds and odours.

There comes the morning with the golden basket in her right hand bearing the wreath of beauty, silently to crown the earth.

And there comes the evening over the lonely meadows deserted by herds, through trackless paths, carrying cool draughts of peace in her golden pitcher from the western ocean of rest.

But there, where spreads the infinite sky for the soul to take her flight in, reigns the stainless white radiance. There is no day nor night, nor form nor colour, and never, never a word.

68

God loves all His creation. Like a mother, He embraces the poet with the rays of the sun. God is pure brightness and infinite peace, but He welcomes the suffering and is moved by their tears.

THY sunbeam comes upon this earth of mine with arms outstretched and stands at my door the livelong day to carry back to thy feet clouds made of my tears and sighs and songs.

With fond delight thou wrappest about thy starry breast that mantle of misty cloud, turning it into numberless shapes and folds and colouring it with hues everchanging.

It is so light and so fleeting, tender and tearful and dark, that is why thou lovest it, O thou spotless and serene. And that is why it may cover thy awful white light with its pathetic shadows.

69

God is the universal soul, present everywhere and in all things. The joy of the Supreme Being is expressed in the beauty and music of nature. The ebb and flow of the sea calls to mind the rhythmic dance of life and death. The poet is proud to be part of the universal and ageless soul.

THE same stream of life that runs through my veins night and day runs through the world and dances in rhythmic measures.

It is the same life that shoots in joy through the dust of the earth in numberless blades of grass and breaks into tumultuous waves of leaves and flowers.

It is the same life that is rocked in the ocean-cradle of birth and of death, in ebb and in flow.

I feel my limbs are made glorious by the touch of this world of life. And my pride is from the life-throb of ages dancing in my blood this moment.

70

The whole of nature is ever on the move. The rushing torrents, the raging storms, and the fast changing seasons symbolise this swift dance of joy. The love and joy of the Creator permeate all things and sustain them.

IS it beyond thee to be glad with the gladness of this rhythm? to be tossed and lost and broken in the whirl of this fearful joy?

All things rush on, they stop not, they look not behind, no power can hold them back, they rush on.

Keeping steps with that restless, rapid music, seasons come dancing and pass away — colours, tunes, and perfumes pour in endless cascades in the abounding joy that scatters and gives up and dies every moment.

God makes man out of a part of Himself. His grief at this sundering is seen in the anguish and tears of His creation which is an illusion that veils God and man from each other. And so man's search for his Maker goes on through endless ages.

THAT I should make much of myself and turn it on all sides, thus casting coloured shadows on thy radiance — such is thy *maya*.

Thou settest a barrier in thine own being and then callest thy severed self in myriad notes. This thy self-separation has taken body in me.

The poignant song is echoed through all the sky in many-coloured tears and smiles, alarms and hopes; waves rise up and sink again, dreams break and form. In me is thy own defeat of self.

This screen that thou hast raised is painted with innumerable figures with the brush of the night and the day. Behind it thy seat is woven in wondrous mysteries of curves, casting away all barren lines of straightness.

The great pageant of thee and me has overspread the sky. With the tune of thee and me all the air is vibrant, and all ages pass with the hiding and seeking of thee and me.

72

God works in the human heart, causing activity, pain and pleasure. He makes man aware of the beauty of creation and makes His devotee worship Him in many and varied forms.

HE it is, the innermost one, who awakens my being with his deep hidden touches.

He it is who puts his enchantment upon these eyes and joyfully plays on the chords of my heart in varied cadence of pleasure and pain.

He it is who weaves the web of this *maya* in evanescent hues of gold and silver, blue and green, and lets peep out through the folds his feet, at whose touch I forget myself.

Days come and ages pass, and it is ever he who moves my heart in many a name, in many a guise, in many a rapture of joy and of sorrow.

73

Genuine freedom does not consist in renunciation but in the fulfilment of one's duties. God fills the world with beauty and delight, and we should enjoy them with grateful hearts. Through service to fellow beings we should sublimate such pleasures into love of beauty and joy in it.

DELIVERANCE is not for me in renunciation. I feel the embrace of freedom in a thousand bonds of delight.

Thou ever pourest for me the fresh draught of thy wine of various colours and fragrance, filling this earthen vessel to the brim.

My world will light its hundred different lamps with thy flame and place them before the altar of thy temple.

No, I will never shut the doors of my senses. The delights of sight and hearing and touch will bear thy delight.

Yes, all my illusions will burn into illumination of joy, and all my desires ripen into fruits of love.

74

It is evening. A woman has to fetch water from a stream. She is not sure of meeting anyone or even of returning home. But she hears the sweet notes of a flute played by a stranger waiting for her in a boat. It is God Himself who urges man to meet Him.

THE day is no more, the shadow is upon the earth. It is time that I go to the stream to fill my pitcher.

The evening air is eager with the sad music of the water. Ah, it calls me out into the dusk. In the lonely lane there is no passer-by, the wind is up, the ripples are rampant in the river.

I know not if I shall come back home. I know not whom I shall chance to meet. There at the fording in the little boat the unknown man plays upon his lute.

75

The human soul comes from the Divine and returns to the Divine. Like a river that irrigates wherever it flows and ultimately merges with the sea, like the fragrant flower that fades and becomes one with the Divine, the human soul journeys on earth till it is united with God.

THY gifts to us mortals fulfil all our needs and yet run back to thee undiminished.

The river has its everyday work to do and hastens through fields and hamlets; yet its incessant stream winds towards the washing of thy feet.

The flower sweetens the air with its perfume; yet its last service is to offer itself to thee.

Thy worship does not impoverish the world.

From the words of the poet men take what meanings please them; yet their last meaning points to thee.

76

The poet surrenders himself totally to the will of God and remembers Him constantly while performing his humble daily duties. He is confident that God will inspire him in all situations. At the end of his earthly course, he will surrender himself to God in perfect humility.

DAY after day, O lord of my life, shall I stand before thee face to face. With folded hands, O lord of all worlds, shall I stand before thee face to face.

Under thy great sky in solitude and silence, with humble heart shall I stand before thee face to face.

In this laborious world of thine, tumultuous with toil and with struggle, among hurrying crowds shall I stand before thee face to face.

And when my work shall be done in this world, O King of kings, alone and speechless shall I stand before thee face to face.

77

*God is our friend and brother who mixes freely
with humble humanity. To love fellow-beings is
to love God. In our oneness with humble people,
we become one with God. Death is not to be
feared, for through it we are re-united with our
Maker.*

I KNOW thee as my God and stand apart
— I do not know thee as my own and come
closer. I know thee as my father and bow
before thy feet — I do not grasp thy hand
as my friend's.

I stand not where thou comest down and
ownest thyself as mine, there to clasp thee to
my heart and take thee as my comrade.

Thou art the Brother amongst my
brothers, but I heed them not, I divide not
my earnings with them, thus sharing my all
with thee.

In pleasure and in pain I stand not by
the side of men, and thus stand by thee. I
shrink to give up my life, and thus do not
plunge into the great waters of life.

78

Imperfect and ignorant men find defects and imperfections in God's creation which is perfect. Not all perceive this unbroken perfection, and many go in search of the "missing stars" that can never be found.

WHEN the creation was new and all the stars shone in their first splendour, the gods held their assembly in the sky and sang "Oh, the picture of perfection! The joy unalloyed!"

But one cried of a sudden — "It seems that somewhere there is a break in the chain of light and one of the stars has been lost."

The golden string of their harp snapped, their song stopped, and they cried in dismay — "Yes, that lost star was the best, she was the glory of all heavens!"

From that day the search is unceasing for her, and the cry goes on from one to the other that in her the world has lost its one joy!

Only in the deepest silence of night the stars smile and whisper among themselves — "Vain is this seeking! Unbroken perfection is over all!"

79

Though we cannot meet God face to face in our earthly life, we should never forget Him. The pain of separation from God and the longing for reunion with Him should be in us constantly.

IF it is not my portion to meet thee in this my life then let me ever feel that I have missed thy sight — let me not forget for a moment, let me carry the pangs of this sorrow in my dreams and in my wakeful hours.

As my days pass in the crowded market of this world and my hands grow full with the daily profits, let me ever feel that I have gained nothing — let me not forget for a moment, let me carry the pangs of this sorrow in my dreams and in my wakeful hours.

When I sit by the roadside, tired and panting, when I spread my bed low in the dust, let me ever feel that the long journey is still before me — let me not forget for a moment, let me carry the pangs of this sorrow in my dreams and in my wakeful hours.

When my rooms have been decked out and the flutes sound and the laughter there is loud, let me ever feel that I have not invited thee to my house — let me not forget for a moment, let me carry the pangs of this sorrow in my dreams and in my wakeful hours.

80

The poet desires intensely for reunion with God. He feels his life is of no use, and longs for divine light to enlighten him, to end his earthly life and to liberate him. He wants to be dissolved in the beauty of nature and become God's plaything and finally become one with Him.

I AM like a remnant of a cloud of autumn uselessly roaming in the sky, O my sun ever-glorious! Thy touch has not yet melted my vapour, making me one with thy light, and thus I count months and years separated from thee.

If this be thy wish and if this be thy play, then take this fleeting emptiness of mine, paint it with colours, gild it with gold, float it on the wanton wind and spread it in varied wonders.

And again when it shall be thy wish to end this play at night, I shall melt and vanish away in the dark, or it may be in a smile of the white morning, in a coolness of purity transparent.

81

God is present and active in nature at all times and in all places. He is kind and loving, and ever seeks our good. If we place our faith and trust in Him, He will do for us what we cannot, and fill us with His bliss.

ON many an idle day have I grieved over lost time. But it is never lost, my lord. Thou hast taken every moment of my life in thine own hands.

Hidden in the heart of things thou art nourishing seeds into sprouts, buds into blossoms, and ripening flowers into fruitfulness.

I was tired and sleeping on my idle bed and imagined all work had ceased. In the morning I woke up and found my garden full with wonders of flowers.

82

God is eternal, but man has only a limited time. As the ages pass, though man forgets Him, He awaits the return of the human soul, His beloved. It is never too late to return to Him, for His patience, love and mercy are infinite.

TIME is endless in thy hands, my lord. There is none to count thy minutes.

Days and nights pass and ages bloom and fade like flowers. Thou knowest how to wait.

Thy centuries follow each other perfecting a small wild flower.

We have no time to lose, and having no time we must scramble for our chances. We are too poor to be late.

And thus it is that time goes by while I give it to every querulous man who claims it, and thine altar is empty of all offerings to the last.

At the end of the day I hasten in fear lest thy gate be shut; but I find that yet there is time.

83

God is the poet's loving mother for whom he will weave a chain out of his pearl-like tears. It is not the offering of material wealth but that of the tears and suffering of the devotee which is a genuine offering; it is valued by God for it purifies the soul and brings it closer to Him.

MOTHER, I shall weave a chain of pearls for thy neck with my tears of sorrow.

The stars have wrought their anklets of light to deck thy feet, but mine will hang upon thy breast.

Wealth and fame come from thee and it is for thee to give or to withhold them. But this my sorrow is absolutely mine own, and when I bring it to thee as my offering thou rewardest me with thy grace.

84

God divided parts of Himself and made out of them this beautiful universe. The pain of this division penetrates the whole of creation and is manifested in the loves and desires, pleasures and pains of human beings.

IT is the pang of separation that spreads throughout the world and gives birth to shapes innumerable in the infinite sky.

It is this sorrow of separation that gazes in silence all night from star to star and becomes lyric among rustling leaves in rainy darkness of July.

It is this overspreading pain that deepens into loves and desires, into sufferings and joys in human homes; and this it is that ever melts and flows in songs through my poet's heart.

85

Worldly wealth is futile. From his heavenly home man comes to this world weak and defenceless. He will return to that home leaving behind all the riches he collected through sweat and toil.

WHEN the warriors came out first from their master's hall, where had they hid their power? Where were their armour and their arms?

They looked poor and helpless, and the arrows were showered upon them on the day they came out from their master's hall.

When the warriors marched back again to their master's hall where did they hide their power?

They had dropped the sword and dropped the bow and the arrow; peace was on their foreheads, and they had left the fruits of their life behind them on the day they marched back again to their master's hall.

Death is God's messenger whom the poet will welcome heartily, offering him all his treasures. But he will reserve his soul, to offer it personally to his Maker.

DEATH, thy servant, is at my door. He has crossed the unknown sea and brought thy call to my home.

The night is dark and my heart is fearful — yet I will take up the lamp, open my gates and bow to him my welcome. It is thy messenger who stands at my door.

I will worship him with folded hands, and with tears. I will worship him placing at his feet the treasure of my heart.

He will go back with his errand done, leaving a dark shadow on my morning; and in my desolate home only my forlorn self will remain as my last offering to thee.

87

In his bereavement and grief, the poet has the sure hope of meeting his beloved in the world of God where all dear ones lost will be found again and all happiness will be restored.

IN desperate hope I go and search for her in all the corners of my room; I find her not.

My house is small and what once has gone from it can never be regained.

But infinite is thy mansion, my lord, and seeking her I have come to thy door.

I stand under the golden canopy of thine evening sky and I lift my eager eyes to thy face.

I have come to the brink of eternity from which nothing can vanish — no hope, no happiness, no vision of a face seen through tears.

Oh, dip my emptied life into that ocean, plunge it into the deepest fullness. Let me for once feel that lost sweet touch in the allness of the universe.

The temple lies in ruins and the idol there is not worshipped. Man makes new idols and soon forgets them. He sets up new ideals and values and then puts them away. This materialistic world neglects the eternal God.

DEITY of the ruined temple! The broken strings of *Vina* sing no more your praise. The bells in the evening proclaim not your time of worship. The air is still and silent about you.

In your desolate dwelling comes the vagrant spring breeze. It brings the tidings of flowers — the flowers that for your worship are offered no more.

Your worshipper of old wanders ever longing for favour still refused. In the eventide, when fires and shadows mingle with the gloom of dust, he wearily comes back to the ruined temple with hunger in his heart.

Many a festival day comes to you in

silence, deity of the ruined temple. Many a night of worship goes away with lamp unlit.

Many new images are built by masters of cunning art and carried to the holy stream of oblivion when their time is come.

Only the deity of the ruined temple remains unworshipped in deathless neglect.

89

Amidst his busy activity, in a moment of sudden, mystical experience the poet hears the call of his divine Lover. Henceforth he will be totally devoted to Him and singing His praises. And all things become beautiful and joyful to him.

NO more noisy, loud words from me — such is my master's will. Henceforth I deal in whispers. The speech of my heart will be carried on in murmurings of a song.

Men hasten to the King's market. All the buyers and sellers are there. But I have my untimely leave in the middle of the day, in the thick of work.

Let then the flowers come out in my garden, though it is not their time; and let the midday bees strike up their lazy hum.

Full many an hour have I spent in the strife of the good and the evil, but now it is the pleasure of my playmate of the empty days to draw my heart on to him; and I know not why is this sudden call to what useless inconsequence!

90

*When death comes, the poet will welcome it,
honour it and offer it all that he has acquired in
life. Through death one is freed from the body
and is able to come face to face with God.*

ON the day when death will knock at thy
door what wilt thou offer to him?

Oh, I will set before my guest the full
vessel of my life — I will never let him go
with empty hands.

All the sweet vintage of all my autumn
days and summer nights, all the earnings
and gleanings of my busy life will I place
before him at the close of my days when
death will knock at my door.

The poet is the bride who awaits her bridegroom, Death. When he comes, she will offer him all her hopes, joys and love. Now the bridegroom has arrived and the wedding is celebrated. As a bride finds fulfilment in her union with the bridegroom, so the poet's life will be fulfilled in union with Death.

O THOU the last fulfilment of life, Death, my death, come and whisper to me!

Day after day have I kept watch for thee; for thee have I borne the joys and pangs of life.

All that I am, that I have, that I hope and all my love have ever flowed towards thee in depth of secrecy. One final glance from thine eyes and my life will be ever thine own.

The flowers have been woven and the garland is ready for the bridegroom. After the wedding the bride shall leave her home and meet her lord alone in the solitude of night.

The poet will die, but nature will go on. As usual, each passing hour will bring its pleasure or pain. As death is near, the poet is concerned with spiritual things and no more with material wealth. Nature makes no distinction between the rich and the poor.

I KNOW that the day will come when my sight of this earth shall be lost, and life will take its leave in silence, drawing the last curtain over my eyes.

Yet stars will watch at night, and morning rise as before, and hours heave like sea waves casting up pleasures and pains.

When I think of this end of my moments, the barrier of the moments breaks and I see by the light of death thy world with its careless treasures. Rare is its lowliest seat, rare is its meanest of lives.

Things that I longed for in vain and things that I got — let them pass. Let me but truly possess the things that I ever spurned and overlooked.

93

Death is calling, and the poet is about to begin his last journey. He thanks his fellow beings, his brothers, for their goodness to him, begs for their good wishes, and leaves to them whatever wealth he has.

I HAVE got my leave. Bid me farewell, my brothers! I bow to you all and take my departure.

Here I give back the keys of my door— and I give up all claims to my house. I only ask for last kind words from you.

We were neighbours for long, but I received more than I could give. Now the day has dawned and the lamp that lit my dark corner is out. A summons has come and I am ready for my journey.

94

The poet is eager to set out on the journey of death. He hopes to meet God, his Beloved, at the end of the journey. He will dress like a bridegroom and go without fearing difficulties and dangers, sure to be welcomed by God.

AT this time of my parting, wish me good luck, my friends! The sky is flushed with the dawn and my path lies beautiful.

Ask not what I have with me to take there. I start on my journey with empty hands and expectant heart.

I shall put on my wedding garland. Mine is not the red-brown dress of the traveller, and though there are dangers on the way I have no fear in my mind.

The evening star will come out when my voyage is done and the plaintive notes of the twilight melodies be struck up from the King's gateway.

95

Life and death are presented here as the two breasts of the Divine Mother. We are born strangers in the world, but this mother nurses us. Birth brings the soul into this strange world; death takes it to the unknown eternity. Taken from one breast, the baby weeps; put to the other, he is consoled. So does man, leaving life, find rest in death.

I WAS not aware of the moment when I first crossed the threshold of this life.

What was the power that made me open out into this vast mystery like a bud in the forest at midnight!

When in the morning I looked upon the light I felt in a moment that I was no stranger in this world, that the inscrutable without name and form had taken me in its arms in the form of my own mother.

Even so, in death the same unknown will appear as ever known to me. And because I love this life, I know I shall love death as well.

The child cries out when from the right breast the mother takes it away, in the very next moment to find in the left one its consolation.

96

The poet gives his parting message. Having experienced the matchless, indescribable divine love in this world, seen God's greatness and glory in the universe and experienced the thrill of His blissful touch, he is now happy to die.

WHEN I go from hence let this be my parting word, that what I have seen is unsurpassable.

I have tasted of the hidden honey of this lotus that expands on the ocean of light, and thus am I blessed — let this be my parting word.

In this playhouse of infinite forms I have had my play and here have I caught sight of him that is formless.

My whole body and my limbs have thrilled with his touch who is beyond touch; and if the end comes here, let it come — let this be my parting word.

God and man play freely together. In his great delight in the play, the poet did not care to learn who his Playmate was or what His songs meant. At times he was aware of the divine presence, but only in late life did he realize that it was with the King of kings that he played.

WHEN my play was with thee I never questioned who thou wert. I knew nor shyness nor fear, my life was boisterous.

In the early morning thou wouldst call me from my sleep like my own comrade and lead me running from glade to glade.

On those days I never cared to know the meaning of songs thou sangest to me. Only my voice took up the tunes, and my heart danced in their cadence.

Now, when the playtime is over, what is this sudden sight that is come upon me? The world with eyes bent upon thy feet stands in awe with all its silent stars.

*God has conquered the poet; he will lay all that
he has at the feet of his Victor and Master, and
there he will weep out his pain. The loving and
merciful God will bless him and call him, and
he will gladly welcome death and go to Him.*

I WILL deck thee with trophies, garlands of
my defeat. It is never in my power to escape
unconquered.

I surely know my pride will go to the
wall, my life will burst its bonds in exceeding
pain, and my empty heart will sob out in
music like a hollow reed, and the stone will
melt in tears.

I surely know the hundred petals of a
lotus will not remain closed for ever and
the secret recess of its honey will be bared.

From the blue sky an eye shall gaze
upon me and summon me in silence.
Nothing will be left for me, nothing
whatever, and utter death shall I receive at
thy feet.

99

The poet who has been in control of his life yields the control to God. All the struggles of man against God's will are of no use. In the pursuit of worldly wealth man forgets the needs of his own spirit. But the poet is preparing for death and waiting for his Master's arrival.

WHEN I give up the helm I know that the time has come for thee to take it. What there is to do will be instantly done. Vain is this struggle.

Then take away your hands and silently put up with your defeat, my heart, and think it your good fortune to sit perfectly still where you are placed.

These my lamps are blown out at every little puff of wind, and trying to light them I forget all else again and again.

But I shall be wise this time and wait in the dark, spreading my mat on the floor; and whenever it is thy pleasure, my lord, come silently and take thy seat here.

100

The ocean of this universe hides in its depths the perfect pearl — God. The poet has ever been searching for this Infinite. He no more enjoys being tossed about by the waves, but is eager to die and become one with the Eternal.

I DIVE down into the depth of the ocean of forms, hoping to gain the perfect pearl of the formless.

No more sailing from harbour to harbour with this my weather-beaten boat. The days are long passed when my sport was to be tossed on waves.

And now I am eager to die into the deathless.

Into the audience hall by the fathomless abyss where swells up the music of toneless strings I shall take this harp of my life.

I shall tune it to the notes of forever, and when it has sobbed out its last utterance, lay down my silent harp at the feet of the silent.

101

*Through his songs, the poet has sought his Maker
all his life. Through his songs he grew in wisdom
and saw the depth of reality. Through his songs
he hopes to reach his final destination — God.*

EVER in my life have I sought thee with my songs. It was they who led me from door to door, and with them have I felt about me, searching and touching my world.

It was my songs that taught me all the lessons I ever learnt; they showed me secret paths, they brought before my sight many a star on the horizon of my heart.

They guided me all the day long to the mysteries of the country of pleasure and pain, and, at last, to what palace gate have they brought me in the evening at the end of my journey?

102

Having had a mystic realisation of God, the poet has tried to depict God in his songs; but he has failed to explain his meaning. Divine presence is a mystic experience that comes through faith; words cannot communicate it. God loves the mystics and comes to them while the world scorns them.

I BOASTED among men that I had known you. They see your pictures in all works of mine. They come and ask me, "Who is he?" I know not how to answer them. I say, "Indeed, I cannot tell." They blame me and they go away in scorn. And you sit there smiling.

I put my tales of you into lasting songs. The secret gushes out from my heart. They come and ask me, "Tell me all your meanings." I know not how to answer them. I say, "Ah, who knows what they mean!" They smile and go away in utter scorn. And you sit there smiling.

103

The poet, fully contented, offers his entire possessions at the feet of God, in an act of final and total surrender. As the stream flows into the sea, the poet's songs will merge with the Eternal. Like cranes resting in their nests, he will rest in his eternal home.

IN one salutation to thee, my God, let all my senses spread out and touch this world at thy feet.

Like a rain-cloud of July hung low with its burden of unshed showers let all my mind bend down at thy door in one salutation to thee.

Let all my songs gather together their diverse strains into a single current and flow to a sea of silence in one salutation to thee

Like a flock of homesick cranes flying night and day back to their mountain nests let all my life take its voyage to its eternal home in one salutation to thee.

INDEX OF FIRST WORDS

177